Read All About
Earthly Oddities

HOT SPRINGS AND GEYSERS

Patricia Armentrout

The Rourke Press, Inc.
Vero Beach, Florida 32964

6835193

PHOTO CREDITS
© Dick Dietrich: Cover, pgs. 16, 19; © Jerry & Barbara Jividen: pgs. 4, 6; © Effie McDermott: pgs. 7, 18, 22; © Jim Kissinger/ Milwaukee Stock: pg. 21; © James P. Rowan: pgs. 12, 13, 15; © Marty Youngmann: pgs. 9, 10

ACKNOWLEDGMENTS
The author wishes to acknowledge David Armentrout for his contribution in writing this book.

Library of Congress Cataloging-in-Publication Data

Armentrout, Patricia, 1960-
    Hot springs and geysers / by Patricia Armentrout.
        p. cm. — (Earthly Oddities)
    Includes index.
    Summary: Explores the nature, location, and causes of hot springs, including those that gush hot water and steam into the air and are called geysers.
    ISBN 1-57103-154-5
    1. Hot springs—Juvenile literature. 2. Geysers—Juvenile literature.
[1. Hot springs. 2. Geysers.]
I. Title II. Series: Armentrout, Patricia, 1960- Earthly Oddities.
GB1198.A86 1996
551.2'3—dc20
                                                                96–2892
                                                                    CIP
                                                                    AC

Printed in the USA

TABLE OF CONTENTS

HOT SPRINGS

A hot spring is a flow of water heated by hot rock underground. The temperature of the water can be a few degrees above the air temperature, or it can be hot enough to boil.

Hot springs are found all over the world; but most are in the United States, New Zealand, Japan, and parts of Russia.

In some parts of the world, steam from large hot springs is used to produce electricity for homes and businesses.

Some hot spring pools have crystal-clear water.

WHAT CAUSES HOT SPRINGS?

Hot springs are usually found near an active or inactive **volcano** (vahl KAY no). Water from rain and snow slowly trickles from the surface deep into the ground. Because hot springs are near areas of volcanic activity, the underground rock is very hot.

The water in hot springs can be warm or in some cases boiling hot.

Water in hot springs usually starts as rain or snow and is heated by hot rock underground.

The water is heated by the hot rock. The heated water then makes its way through a channel back to the surface in the form of a hot spring.

SWIM OR STAY AWAY?

Small pools of heated water sometimes form around hot springs. These pools can be very inviting to swimmers. The warm waters can be a sort of natural hot tub. Owners of some large hot springs even charge admission from visitors wanting to take a relaxing swim.

Some hot springs are perfectly safe to swim in—but some can be deadly. Poisonous gas may be present in some hot springs. Drinking the water or even smelling the fumes from these springs can kill humans and animals.

Public pools of hot spring water attract many visitors each year.

MINERAL-RICH WATER

Hot spring water naturally dissolves rocks in and around the spring. This process leaves large amounts of **minerals** (MIN er ulz) in the water.

It has long been thought that mineral-rich hot springs can cure some health problems. The city of Hot Springs, Arkansas, attracts visitors for this reason. Nearly two million people of all ages soak in the hot spring water every year.

A cloud of steam rises from this hot spring.

FUMAROLES AND MUD POTS

A **fumarole** (FYOO muh rol) is a hot spring with very little water. The water is so hot that most all of it boils away and only steam and gas erupt at the surface. The steam has been found to reach temperatures greater than 230 degrees.

Hot steam escapes from these fumaroles.

Mud pots are sunken fumaroles.

Mud pots are fumaroles that have sunken below the surface. Gases and chemical reactions form an acid that causes the hot rock to dissolve. A wet clay is created. In the spring, when more moisture is in the air, mud pots can be thin and runny. By the fall, mud pots can completely dry up and become a fumarole again.

GEYSERS

Geysers (GY zerz) are hot springs that shoot hot water and steam into the air. The word "geyser" comes from Iceland. It means to "gush forth."

Some geysers spew water only a few inches above the ground. Large geysers can throw water and steam hundreds of feet into the air.

Most geysers don't gush water and steam all the time. Instead they erupt at **intervals** (IN ter vulz). The time between eruptions can vary from minutes to weeks to even months.

Geysers throw water and steam into the air at intervals.

WHAT CAUSES GEYSERS?

Water in a geyser is heated by the same volcanic heat that warms other hot springs. A geyser erupts because very hot water is trapped under pressure in a chamber below the surface. The deepest water gets so hot that it explodes into steam.

The steam forces its way through channels in the geyser and erupts at the surface. The explosion of the steam and water empties most of the water in a geyser chamber. After the eruption, the water drains back into the geyser and the entire process begins again.

Great Fountain Geyser shoots water and steam high into the air.

YELLOWSTONE NATIONAL PARK

Perhaps the most famous hot spring and geyser area in the world is Yellowstone National Park. Yellowstone covers areas in Idaho, Montana, and Wyoming. The park contains about 2,000 geysers and more than 10,000 hot springs—more than any place on Earth.

Bison roam freely among the geysers in Yellowstone National Park.

Castle Geyser is surrounded by small pools of spring water.

Yellowstone Park is actually a huge collapsed volcano. The volcano erupted about 600,000 years ago. The rock deep below the volcano will stay very hot for a million years or more. This hot rock is the source that heats Yellowstone's many geysers and hot springs.

FAMOUS GEYSERS

Imagine a column of steam and water shooting over 1500 feet into the air. That is higher than the Empire State Building. It happened at a geyser named Waimangu, in New Zealand, between 1902 and 1905.

The most famous geyser in the United States is Old Faithful in Yellowstone National Park. It erupts about every 65 minutes, shooting water and steam 150 feet into the air.

Grand Geyser, also in Yellowstone, is probably the park's most magnificent geyser. It sends water over 200 feet high about three times a day.

Old Faithful Geyser is famous for its regular eruption of water and steam.

GLOSSARY

fumarole (FYOO muh rol) — a hole in the earth's surface from which hot steam escapes

geysers (GY zerz) — hot springs that shoot steam and water into the air

intervals (IN ter vulz) — spaces or periods of time between events

minerals (MIN er ulz) — natural substances from the earth such as coal, quartz, gold, and salt

volcano (vahl KAY no) — an opening in Earth's surface where steam and lava erupt

Grand Geyser spouts a fountain of water over 200 feet high.

INDEX